Copyright © 2022 Michèle Saint-Michel
All rights reserved.
10 9 8 7 6 5 4 3 2 1

Published by Bad Saturn. BAD SATURN and associated logos are trademarks and/ or registered trademarks.

All rights reserved under International and Pan-American Copyright Conventions. No part of this publication may be reproduced, transmitted, downloaded, decompiled, reverse engineered, or stored in or introduced into any information storage and retrieval system, in any form or by any means, whether electronic or mechanical, now known or hereafter invented, without the express written permission of the publisher. For information regarding permissions, email Bad Saturn, Attention: Permissions Department.

The publisher does not have any control over and does not assume any responsibility for author or third-party websites or their content.

LIBRARY OF CONGRESS
CATALOGING-IN-PUBLICATION DATA

Saint-Michel, Michèle.
Experiments in Dreaming: A Lined Journal
/ by Michèle Saint-Michel.
— 1st ed.
p.
Crn.
ISBN: 978-0-9999020-4-2

Summary:
A lined journal with room for dreams. Based on the work of artist and poet Michèle Saint-Michel, this lined journal creates space for jotting down thoughtful notes, reimaginings, and plans. For anyone who dreams of pulling a better world into existence.

In me the caresser of life
I believe in those wing'd
purposes,

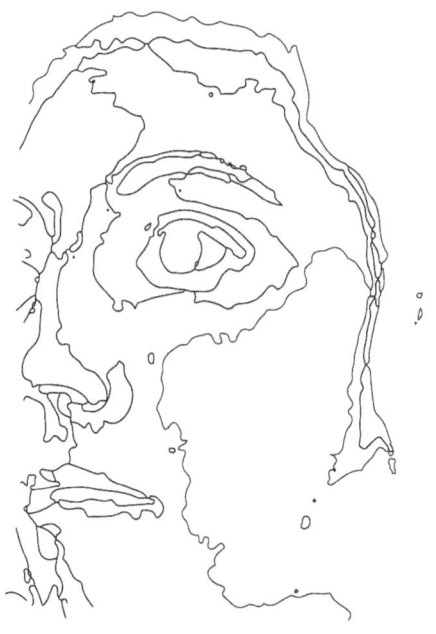

And again as I walk'd
the beach under
　　　　the paling stars
　　of morning.

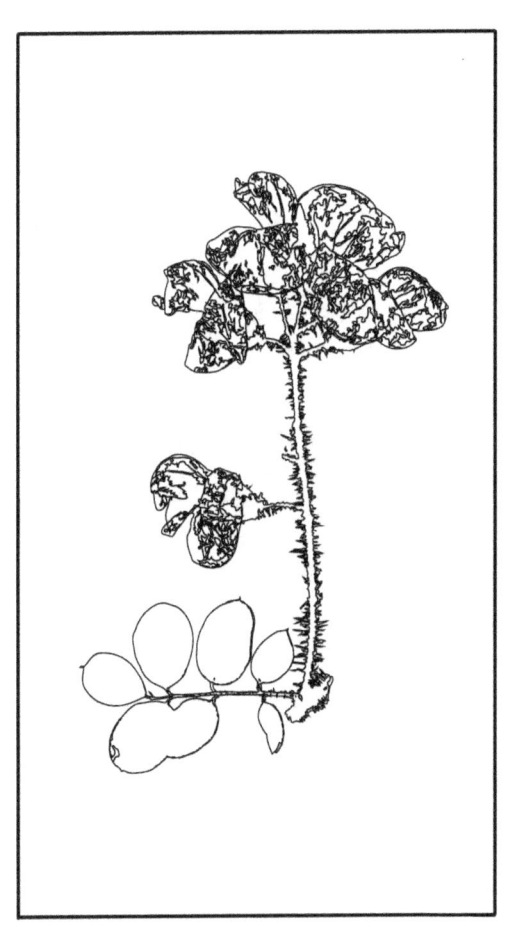

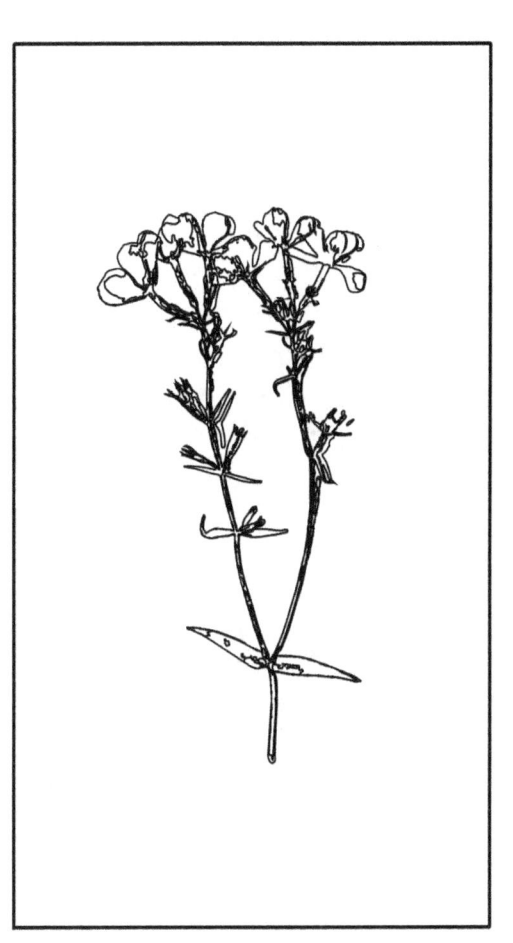

Space and Time!
  now I see it is true,
what I guess'd at,
What I guess'd when I loaf'd on the grass,
What I guess'd while I lay alone in my bed,
And again as I walk'd the beach
    under
        the
            paling
        stars
      of
          morning.

a lined journal with room for dreams

For anyone who dreams of pulling a better world into existence, this lined journal creates space for thoughts, notes, and plans.

...

This collection of journals is punctuated by the words of Walt Whitman. The poet's work is a pillar of Saint-Michel's erasure and concrete poetry collection, *Saint Agatha Mother Redeemer*. Working closely with the text created an intimacy in particular with his magnum opus, *Leaves of Grass*. Though it was first published in 1855, Whitman spent most of his professional life writing and rewriting the epic work. Take a page from Whitman and continue writing and rewriting your own story.

Buy or gift Michèle Saint-Michel's books to experience words and worlds with new eyes.

...

Also by Michèle Saint-Michel

A Journal of Gigantic Beauty

Journeywork of the Stars

Grief Is an Origami Swan

Saint Agatha Mother Redeemer

Saint Agatha Mother Redeemer Coloring Book

Liner Notes for Getting Out Without Catching Fire

www.ingramcontent.com/pod-product-compliance
Lightning Source LLC
Chambersburg PA
CBHW070432010526
44118CB00014B/2013